You'll be Fast as Lightning Coveting My Painted Tail

Poems

Also by Toni Thomas:

Chosen
    Brick Road Poetry Press

Fast as Lightening
    Gribble Press

Walking on Water
    Finishing Line Press

Blue Halo
    Annalese Press

Ace Raider of the Unfathomable Universe
    Annalese Press

You'll be Fast as Lightning Coveting My Painted Tail

Toni Thomas

First published in 2017 by Annalese Press
134 Towngate
Netherthong
Holmfirth
West Yorkshire HD9 3XZ
England

Copyright © 2017 Toni Thomas

Please Note
All characters and situations appearing
in these pages are in the service of poetry.
Any resemblance to real persons,
living or dead, is purely coincidental.

All rights reserved. No part of this publication may be reproduced, stored, or transmitted in any form, or by any means electronic, mechanical or photocopying, recording or otherwise, without the express written permission of the publisher.

Cover and interior artwork by Peter Wadsworth
Cover painting: *Ophelia* (1894) John Waterhouse.
Private collection

British Library Cataloguing-in-Publication Data
A catalogue record for this book is available on request from the British Library.

ISBN 978-0-9956652-3-1

Acknowledgments

Grateful acknowledgement is made to the editors of the following publications in which some of these poems first appeared (in slightly different versions):

Bellevue Literary Review:
"How Many Times Has My Good Luck Ring"

Haight Ashbury Literary Journal:
"Tribute"
"We Query the Past"

North Dakota Quarterly:
"I Want to Knit You Socks"
"The Man on the Bus"

Poem: "My Mother Offered Me"

Rhino: "I am Impregnated"

Weber: The Contemporary West:
"Back in Yevsky You Came to me"
"At 8pm I will Meet My Lover"

Winner 2010 Gribble Press Chapbook Poetry Prize

Contents

Part One: *Appetite*

I will marry you	1
Will you come to me	3
Appetite	4
I want to knit you socks	6
For as long as I can remember	7

Part Two: *Twice Exiled*

In the Immaculate Conception Church	8
In the book of my mother's love	10
I was twelve when I learnt about sin	11
When the wind lurched	13
I hold the globe	15
When the first bug conquered the next	16
In September triumph struts around	18
All her life	19
My mother offered me	20

Part Three: *A Subversion of Slinky Dresses*

My mother came here	22
The valley of my love	24
I stockpile midnight	25
I am impregnated	27
Tribute	28

We walk through cedar	29
When you query the papers	31
I am counting luck	32

Part Four: *Impervious to the World*

The lip closed five times	34
A Season of Praise	36
We query the past	38
Oaks Park Fairground	39
I gather the hairnets of my life	40
The man on the bus	42
For as long as I can remember	43

Part Five: *Tiny Wings on her Fingers*

Girl cloaked in thin cotton	45
We puncture the orange all over	46
I apostrophe everything	48
If I cloak the world	49
It is November	50
A stranger lives in my shoes	51
It is Late	52
He said she had wings on her fingers	53
I will not be paraded	55

Part Six: *Jewels on a Serpent Ring*

We paper chain loops of colored paper	57
I staple cotton	59
We dollop whipped cream	60
Back in Yevsky you came to me	61
You keep track	63
When I go through the chronicles	64

Summer sits with its dry tongue	66
Morning is an arm of light	68
Precocious girl	69

PART SEVEN: *Perfect Pantomime*

At 8pm I will meet my lover	70
Lucky in love the cards tell her	71
How many times has my good luck ring	73
You lead with your lusts flailing	74
Summer sits	76
When my Prince Comes he will be as Fast as Lightning	77
If you eat a perfect peach	78
In October I will marry you when the jewels hang on the leafless tree	79

girl with knots in her hair
a mission trellis
that stopgaps the rain

leave me here wandering
the parasitical versions of paradise
that paw at my heels

listening to the wind in the field
the plover not shrew
in the jade tree

listening to you

Part One

Appetite

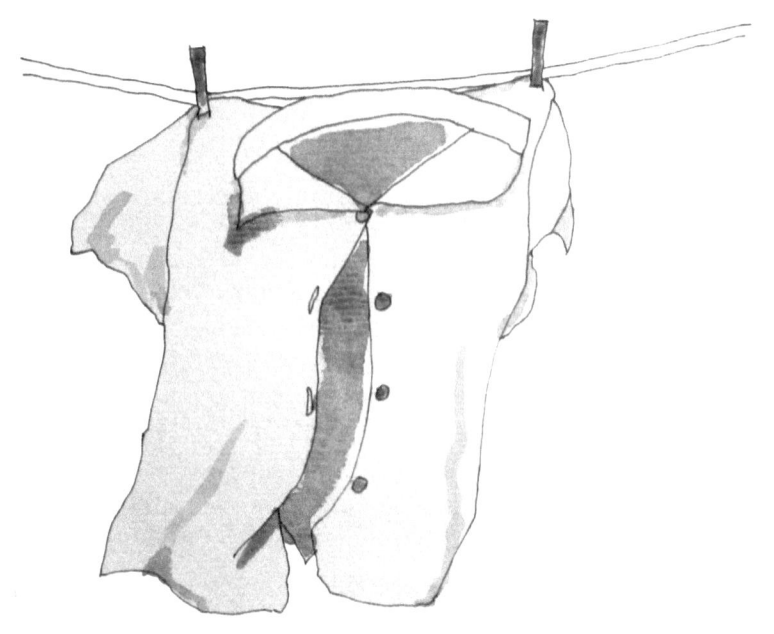

I will marry you

when the clothesline eats her lament
swaying above the green bayed yard.

You are carnivorous.
It's not like you to proposition want
make a pact
your mock tuxedo over an ice blue shirt
the garden a swell of eucalyptus
fireweed bleeding purple above the
nasturtiums' loose skin.

I could curse my luck or bless it
for the mess I am in -
my body floating on foam
in the green bayed yard
the clothesline a dangle of dungarees
lamentation, loose eyelet
below the moon's strict gaze.

I stand here
laurel infested
the labor of how many soaked tea leaves
fairy tales
girlish infested shoes.

A few months from now
autumn will find me
with its eye for justice, scissored leaves.
Our food will be hoisted up between trees.
We will want to devour our past
not know how.
I will sway my hips to the invisible
samba playing in my head.

You will eat fitfully.
Rehearse your love for me.
Examine the pacts we have made.
Argue them away
til they are a burial ground
fresh with three fisted rain.

My own laments
inscrutable as the field grass

burning.

Will you come to me

when I am broken branches
and the night has escaped
with my shoes?

They say it takes three score years
to know yourself
stop waxing your legs.

I am the interceptor of snatched shoes
crooked hems
words the tongue squeezes with a
merciless fist.

If I eat vetch
will I become
a slowed commotion
the way-station for flies
the sky's unseasonable tumbling

can a girl with three used up lives
be pasted back
find repose in the fireweed's indecent burning
the cucumber's prickly body pregnant
in the shade under the vine leaves?

When I cross the path to happiness
will it speak to me as a snake
devouring the mouse in the field
or bend me into another kind of being
who hears the collapse of the wind
the sun's vigilance
lozenges hope
knows the climate of
her own burning?

Appetite

I keep gobbling mercy
like crème cakes that never give up
flirtatious hours
a view of your arms no longer
estimating the rain

have a habit of losing things—
my mother's notebooks, coat pins
slug infested nasturtium
the lozenge tin stuffed with my children's hair
clever men with too much bust.

In July moles hound the dirt in our yard
pile it into mounds
I turn up an old spoon, glass shards
the grass's over enameled face
want to flag down the moon
search my past
the terrible weight
dungarees on a buckled clothesline.

You hound me with the practical mien
of happiness you hive in your hands
the day's loose tongue
the watering can's deliverance
swamp of mosquitoes that
loiter our bed.

They say the moon can go anywhere
with her curved tail
mercy hangs in sloped trees
a deserted corn field.

You grow slant in moonlight.
We hardly see each other.

I thrash around in the dark
become just a gnat on your door
the apostrophe with a vacant end.

God—are you a flashlight
in the fallow field
disguised feet
a handrail only the most collapsed
beings can hold
the tiny insect who impregnates
the snow?

I want to knit you socks

soft mohair
blue as jays against a fleet of trees
let you be the squire
of the squared off carpet thread.

It is October.
My fingers lament summer's easy shoes
the way want never carved a hole in midnight
my dead forsythia, paled begonia.

You need candlelight and warm feet.
I know you need more than this
but we are not saying.
It is easy to live on promises
the hope of deliverance.
You plastic wrap the parlor windows
seal them tight
want to sit without drafts.

I am a fish in a small bowl
examine the thickness
my webbed tail
the way hairline cracks seep

the exquisite anguish
of feeling so secure
in such a tempered glass world.

For as long as I can remember

you have wanted to dine with me
rip up the floorboards.
Pregnant, barefoot
I carry your sanguine wishes
calypso orchids
into the halt of spring
become the rosary
of blue glass

eat alone
let the afternoon light save
am dissolution in a pot of juice
the early wedding ceremony
where the bride eats
the apricot cake before her time.

I am lured by many things
refined by the gold nuggets
the world brazens
wait on that rap from your door
am stubborn as a shelf of sin
hell bent day.

It is hard to tell what will become of me.

Part Two

Twice Exiled

In the Immaculate Conception Church

the mahogany pews shine
bright as rattleless children
my mother looks almost obedient
in her crinkled rayon, spike heels
bullet holes.
Men eye her shapely legs
imagine another kind of heaven.

She tells me that faith saves
nothing can rinse God's favor
from my hair.
I become the altar of her love
devour my father's fence lines
the busted screen door
boxed angel cake
till I am porcelain in my smooth smock
silent, blameless
latched to the corner playing with dolls.

There is a loneliness that reinvests itself
on sodden wheels
a God so fierce nothing claims us
but the tailgates of a strict happiness.

I travel through schools
run amuck in the strident machinery
get big then small
so small almost nobody sees me
write poems handcuffed to the wind
watch you chain linked to rush hour
the weight of clotheslines, cappuccino
the beehives of happiness that circle a mall.

In the Immaculate Conception Church
you hold the baby as if he'll never
desert you
there will be no famine in the world
no one speaks words sharpened
with the retinol of knives.

I wear worship
a girl's unransomed prayer book
white frock rehearsed around gold braiding.

In the book of my mother's love

there are many pinholes
watercolors seeded on grey days
shoes with sorry laces
a pebbled sole.

I peel hope out of the sideboard
slice through grapefruit
on the poinsettia drenched table
remember her herculean strength
that hoisted the oak hutch
dragged couches
rearranged rooms.

My father recites newspaper columns—
the cloning of chickens
boy with the torn arm
who navigates missiles
Easter miracles arriving in
somebody else's back yard
the pink and green color trend
that will consecrate spring.
He doesn't know yet my mother will die.

You promise to be everything
sizzle and ice, calypso orchid and thistle
angel trumpet poisonous as sin
with its affable scent bleeding
purveyor of the world's truant hold
not antiseptic but soothing
as you roll down my throat
set up white death
some cake batter smooth deliverance
that will later go vanishing away.

I was twelve when I learned about sin

the travesty of shifting beds
the way want scours
sets up its own kind of red faced machinery.
My mother let all of the pigeons
out of their coops on the roof that year
staked out a hole in her bedroom
sank there, pajama clad
with her flurry of breadcrumbs
dark hands.

We can get boney thin before there is
nothing left of us.

My father is a steel spire
circles heaven
never wears God in his shoes
sabotages the toast on our plate
can't ride a bicycle
remembers the nuns in the orphanage
their pure white faces
above the stomp of their
orthopedic shoes.

To conquer heaven do we need
inflammable socks
the brute force of firm doctrine
welded to our lips
do the faltering ones always die here
become unseasonable birds
staple their wings
to winter's lost song?

It is autumn.
The wind so hoarse I can barely hear
my voice in it.
The leaves fluttering in the yellow
and red shawl death brings
my mother's pincushions folded.

Stalwart birds
make a profusion of nests
in the bare branched tree
impervious
their wings pinned to nothing
but the sky's maul
your blue blue hold.

When the wind lurched

I wasn't ready to lean in
not like George M. whose legs collapsed
after swing shift on our way to the car
my sixteen year when I was working
at the paper box factory and the foreman's
back order sheet never dwindled away.
A few years later my mother's legs
buckled from under her
they said it was heart failure
her blue willow tea cup splattered
across the parquet.

Some of us learn to take our stalwart devotion
conquer the day
write treatises on good penmanship
perfectly folded sheets
never panic, leak the lack of love.
Nail the cross to every day.

My brother and I are enterprising
three jobs during college, bushels of apples
my mother's letterpress version of happiness
her sheer nylon stockings that in the end
barely managed to heave themselves up her legs
my father's dark eye encrusting the secret
on every slice of bread.

Is it possible to outlive our own usefulness
buckle because the wind seizes
apostrophe want till it waits sullen by the back door?
My dolls defy the laws of man
hang on with their beautiful stuffed throats

They do not want to be keyboarded away
swept inside till the dust claims.

My daughter erects tiny parasols.
My brother hovers between long work hours
crack's dissolution.
Somewhere a blue windsock veers on a taut clothesline.
I want to kiss you
keep from losing what might stumble
prepare a bed
lounge in the smooth of it, erased edges
the grapevine's seedy.

When the wind lurches
do not ask me to turn away.

I hold the globe

something perishable that can break
like the smashed house
love me, love me not petals
my father plucks
as if life is a dice roll
hard ball pummeled across concrete
place where our runt pup
survives almost three weeks
on syringes of milk
stays warmed invalid
in the cup of my mother's blue hands.

I measure girth
the crawl of continents, sleepy rivers
my son's X mark over Scotland with his red pen
the fact that down the road we may
may not be here
trafficking in rifle restraint
the mercury of dead fish
hemorrhage of want in an overindulged world.

It is August.
Everything wants to fly off
now that the sun claims.
Nasturtium paw out past the lip
of the cottonwoods
weekend hallelujahs revive the retreat center
honeysuckle climbs our porch eave
high heeled shoes carry us
over the day's remises
promise everything
with their kid glove
red lipped desertion
irresistible shine.

When the first bug conquered the next

and the next
and you said that each thing devours
what can't be born
I grew sullen as disused shoes
as people without enough claim
who barter with the night's crowded feet.

In every season my son's old science book says
the planet must have enough light
for plants to live on.
In his experiment all the marigold, cabbage starts
die in the darkened room
while the asters flourish under
the grow lamp's bleached gaze.
For months he has been home schooled
corrals no stopwatch for his brain.

One day will we live in a guileless world
with no strife towing
will the weak be rubbed clean by a cavalier hand
my children field their way past voracity
to ease what can't be born?

I am barefoot in the garden
minding all manner of things.
It is July.
Not a time to fall apart with shrunken wings.
My children, the beets, hole infested cabbage leaves
rows of cos lettuce
even the slug colonies
need me
the dependable watering can of my hands.

This afternoon my children will ride in and out
of the yard pool.
Inflatable as the day's loose skin.
It is summer.
I want to believe we can do anything
go anywhere without the sky falling.

In September triumph struts around

on perilous knees
doesn't talk to strangers
as if dying is a work of art
red and gold sequins
my father's arrested eye
gathering fallen leaves
swelled chestnuts
before sweeping them away.

Is it possible to grow tender
in September's mauling
keep the fierce wind at bay
walk around almost herculean
in your summer toe shoes
indifference to sin
cross burning?

I spit death out
the one my lover devours
with his sodden hands
watch him move away from me
my father's sensuous eye burning.

I want to say there are girls wading
in a blue pool, unsullied geese
that what we love need not desert us
like children who hairpin the moon
fasten jeweled nightingales to the tree
grow easy inside the dark's singing.

All her life

my mother tried to find
a single pair of decent shoes
with wings on them
patronized many stores
painted her toenails dark
as God's love
died too young in a morning embrace
with a blue pagoda
torpedoed our floor
all her serial versions of happiness
thick as snow.

It is September.
I wear shoes brown as sin
stretch out in the yard
let my body lounge in the nasturtium's hymn book
imagine the color of your love.

I know infinity is a glass foot
that God clutches children
plays handball
squires the garden's symphonies
squeezes them all snug
till they are gone.

My mother offered me

the solstice of summer
ground the rain down
rattled in her seersucker dress
across September's damp days
as if vagrancy
her St. Jude prayer book
could save
offer up the world's jackpots
the undefeatable
remove the tyrant of loneliness
staked out by our door.

When I imagine heaven it is a
waxen vessel with its sheen missing
the angels have trouble getting out of their bed
nobody purges paradise with the
knife edge of their blade.

Some things slip away -
silver lockets, good hands, parrots that repeat
some things get stuck
embed themselves in cellophane.
Sometimes we have to look for a steady pulse
in the most uncompromising places.

My son likes magic tricks
tells me there are magicians
who eat up the dark
plant marshmallow skies where
ravens prey
that a magician's hands are elliptical
the moon's half face

know how to take hold of things—
swords, rabbits, scantily clad women—
squeeze them into tight spaces
make things vanish on the bent syllable
of a wave.
Is invisibility a miracle in the right hands?

Before she died, my mother harangued everyone
over the weight of their days
set up a missionary box not for paupers
but for magicians
prayed they would resurrect some forgotten sack
map us with new hands
a complexion for roses
the thistle's simple exuberance.

I hold a cinder box up to the moon
my mantra against dissolution
hope that one day she will find me
not dying of loneliness
but drizzling
one more small miracle
out of the day's blue girth.

Part Three

A Subversion of Slinky Dresses

My mother came here

with her pink fusion shoes
corner of happiness that jabbed
the regular forecast of rain.

Everything comes down to beauty
she said to me with her summer hands
scooped white slip
pink pelicans
the hackneyed version of paradise
she tore down with the lawn's neat edge.

I hold a pocket flashlight
dig death out of the side yard.
Examine it with my blue eye
decide not everything
comes to something in this world
my rear ended car
the crippled cabbage leaves
slug devoured peonies
our black dog who drags his tumored body
toward midnight on half paralyzed legs.
Is anything ever an unequivocal
journey of kisses
smooth tableau the season writes on
with decent hands?

I want to make my yes's and no's
count for something
reek of jasmine, mud flats
become incandescent
as if our faces can speak for us
not Botox perfect
but tenable

as the fireflies steady light
my lover's erased ambivalence
the way my mother's faith
wielded her through bands of cosmos
the terrible lost days
till they accumulated on a durable clothesline
her body never exiled
from the lace underpinnings
in which she was laid.

The valley of my love

harbors shrubs so thick
they deny the ascendancy of rain.
The eye of the heart eavesdrops on loneliness
then walks away.
You nibble goat cheese, dine on chopped liver
the supremacy of words with no sides missing.
We rinse the calloused day from our hair.

My love for you is a subversion of slinky dresses
gone wrong peroxided hair
slumped towns in Maine
where my life longs to lounge
on consonant clotheslines.

Not everything comes to us with equitable claim.
You grind tomatoes into sauce
 brew beer, perch on the porch steps
shriek your evening homily into the night's damp fist.
I snowball love, the parables that herald selflessness
as if the moon's opal tongue won't save
nor my girlish legs over which
the slope of the night's purse empties.

In the belly of the world's platitudes
my mother has lost her noble hands
rises on stilts to keep the lamps burning.
I dust rose flecked plates
cups embedded with blue pagodas
imagine September's loose hair
a picnic blanket loitering
your love for me
imagine your hands taking a detour
past nomenclature
mining the intricate boxed china
I have saved.

I stockpile midnight

with a kept tongue
my glitter clips anchored to my hair
the canvas beach chair squandering
its body across the back lawn
as if vagrancy counts for something
its uncalculated mien
my mother spooling mercy
out of the day's crimped sleeves.
She never apostrophized the moon
stormed her way through it
with a shaved tongue.

Dissolution breeds its own kind of handrails.
The salvation choir's rapt imperialism
God riding impermeable through
every dust storm
heaven impaled on a toothpick
that never grows old.

August nudges with her gold wristbands
perfectly matched teeth.
Do I need to be saved
from my own faulty devices
stowed away
in a cedar chest with ancient dishes
crocheted doilies
wedged in with locks of my sister's hair
the toy monkey that outlived
our playfulness
the kangaroo with the ripped pouch?

Some people squirm through space
become almost invisible
a gnat on God's screen door

the thimble that defuses pinpricks
a night so inscrutable you can hold it up
with your bare hands
keep the sky from falling.

I am impregnated

with five castoff shoes
two pairs and an odd remnant.
The city has shabby rooms.
They are coal fires burning behind
a perfect grate.
Sometimes my life goes missing.
Permeable girls who disappear
summer evenings
dangle their legs
when the tongue of the river
can't get enough.

Lucretius says *infinity*
is a glass slipper
with unceremonious roses
that street lamps burn forever
inside the warmth of the bulb's gaze
burn past the night's flint black hold.
What we bind to us lives on
in the mercy of our hands.

I cupboard glass jars
spawn a storehouse of children
make the night a matchstick
of prayer burning
lounge in my lover's body
as if longing can couple soup cans
erase my mother's early dismissal
the stockpile of kisses
she saved for me.

Tribute

You juggle envelopes
café drinks, blue sheets
your two children.
There is no man
to light the candle
take up their homework
coddle banged up knees.

You will be everything
mercury and water
snowflake cookies
the nursery room and basinet
remedy for colds
assembler of dress hems
snack bars, boxed lunches
bagels with cream cheese
the deli spit-roasted chicken
bagged and carted away.

Your children will love you
grow up, move away.
All day your tired limbs rock climb
attempt to reinvent April
keep the dark at arm's length
never go bust.

We walk through cedar

hemlock
when they die
the stricken trunks spawn moss
fledgling limbs emerge from
the stumps of the once mighty.
This coastal forest never just buries its dead.

We are leashed to two dogs.
Circle the beach, pass headlands.
The sky has its blue shirt on.
The children lug sand toys
a Frisbee, wave boards.
I could count my life by them
circumvent our love for each other
till moonlight is only a scratch on the wall
the stars just pinpricks of creosote burning.

This is our final day.
I am wearing my paisley skirt
from the Goodwill store.
You have decided to change out of your four day old tee
sport linen pants, a crisp blue shirt
hand me your expensive camera
ask me to take a picture of you
Gentleman Quarterly style
hands slid casual in your pockets
as you pose beside the dunes.
I take two shots
let my mind pause on the curiosity of why
you only take my picture
when I am a windswept mess
maneuvering sandy blankets
lunchmeat, a plastic spade.

Our children glide across the waves
slide down sand hills
the dogs run on the beach till they drop.

Hours later after the trays of pizza
children zipped in their sleeping bags
tent windows closed
dogs walked
the beach waits
its canopy of stars
arm of silver spangle
quarter mile down the slope.

I have slipped out of my paisley skirt
want to lead you down that trail
the one you refuse
with your blue voice

imagine how many couples have
made love on nights like this
huddled beside beach fires
the wine cooler tipped in the sand
whispered odd stories
snuggled under blankets
unashamed
playing chord after chord
the hum of their bodies sweet trail
back to happiness calling.

When you query the papers

to see if I am gone
vanished in thin air
a magician's slight of hand on a humid day

when you comb through the want ads
the compost bin with its shredded leaves
moldy melon rind
bedroom's lavender tongue

smugly pack the lace undies
carved wood angel with the naked breasts
the this's and that's which constitute a life
dislodge what sat disguised here

will you wake up suddenly
on a day not unlike this one
miraculous
unbeknown to yourself

wings on your pocked feet
your mind so free
it can hold anything

the light
the garter snake in the field
ambitions that were crushed
your child's hesitant hand

the weeds insistent conferencing
day's repose on a wounded sail

glorious
risen and fallible

fallen even as the rain.

I am counting luck

like a hoard of pennies
a sheepskin purse
as if someday I will survive
my rusted hands
my penchant for telegraphing loneliness
into the weakest shade.

September has come
the desertion of children
to classrooms, dance classes
our three eggplant slumped under the
weight of cold nights
the pumpkin vine threatening
never to come back.

Has it taken nearly forty years
to survive the hard stick of want
in a slim fast world?
Will I wake up one day no longer
an unforecast tree
pregnant with myself
lean like a whippoorwill into the wind's
slant breath
scrawl poems beside the radiator's hissing
the cat's afternoon indifference to me?

Darling - it is so small an exchange
between happiness and dissolution.
Sometimes I feel the boot soles of
your breath
your hands
your terribly big hands that
collapse longitudes

long to avow me of
dissolution
my arms so tenuous
ethereal
the way you set anchor
over my body's soft weight.

Part Four

Impervious to the World

The lip closed five times

on the house of desire
till I said I would rip it up
call myself tepid as tea leaves

wanted to be impervious
skate on ice so thick you
never break through
dislodge the hands of God
from my breath.

Seasons lament of what's not spent
the dog loses hope someone will come
squash vines wither under the averted gaze
my love for you grows fragile
stick thin in moonlight
a tapestry someone
hastily pinned to the wall.

It is Saturday.
Your body is muscular
gorgeous in its naked
as you brush your teeth
move from drawer to drawer
gather the things of the day.
You don't notice me watching
don't know that sometimes desire
dislodges sane things
slinks in disguised feet
gutted lunch pails, snipped time
the children's crayons.

Late night you will water
the vegetable beds, nasturtium

pull the cover taut over the wade pool
scan the internet, drink red wine
down the basement.

At 2am I will wake
feel the empty side of our bed
search for you with my summer hands
hands that have learned
not to ask for much
in the private nature
pressed linens
of your world.

A Season of Praise

My father tells me that the evangelists
have been *taken by faith*
and I imagine a hand swooping down
nothing the same afterwards.

We live beneath the shoulder of
the Christian Retreat Center
below heavy clapping, tidy hymns
retreats that bring late night testimonial
red hot redemption.

Does God ever cure us with a tenuous hand
is it possible to walk to heaven on a gravel road
seeded in dead wisteria, muffled headlights
fractious hands?

Will the world come apart in the talc of my voice
be sewn back together
a sturdy quilt
decent lamp
we can steer by?

I paint icons of Mary
cover my walls in them
not because God has deserted me
but because I decided that somebody
needs to temper him.

They say leavened bread flounders
with too much yeast.
I want to rise so high I can look
in wonder at the diminished earth

hover above the Christian Retreat Center
Northwest cedar, pillars of rain
and be gone.

Will anyone remember
the shy slant of my words
the lean box tree
dissolution we met with a steady gaze?

Will my father's words come back
untainted as July sun
seize me as some people's faith does
my mother no longer grown thin
at the side window
her hollyhock a stubborn
season of praise
in a time of wintering?

We query the past

place a microscope up to the old picture albums -
our faces less angular amid the backyard roses
the young man with no clenched fist
the girl victorious in her cut out crown.

Imagine we were pampered back then
you lived on pound cake, no hastily flung kisses
I stampeded through mud puddles
was permitted to wander every swollen field
salvage yard debris, the diseased elm
find what goes missing.

In February the Northwest jeers
with its grey teeth, fierce rain.
We pray for miracles—
a truant storm that blinds the field
lays white where want is.

You become the tyrant prince in green sleeves.
I live on tinsel hope, dime store romance
am the girl searching paw prints in the snow
slide on ice so thin it may not carry me.

There are damp buns in our hands.
The taper candles refuse to light.
I am easily distracted by your bed
as if imposition has its price to pay
and we are twice exiled
you and I
from the welcoming forest
we could call home.

Oaks Park Fairground

Curlicue potatoes
pinstripe awnings the color of candy
the old dance pavilion boarded up
with secular wings
my sweated palm alone
in the grip of your hand
you who like shaved legs
pare down a girl's whimsy
till it is orderly as baseball stadiums
the past with its yanked teeth
no stray splinters towing.

I snatch potatoes from your wax bag
let the cues curl in my hand
like question marks that never need answering
the toes of curved shoes
the road glitter queen
eyelashes the woman
up in the fifth floor apartment
embellishes for her man.

I know I will do nothing
to tantalize your breath
remember the blonde woman
in the 1948 film
who implored *let us be lovers*
with her sad Hiroshima face.

Have I arrived at the curb
an abbreviation of my once self
rueful as the witch who whittles
spite out of her fallen orchard?

I gather the hairnets of my life

like poor relations
distant cousins
estranged from the sun.
It is September.
Time to take stock of the garden
eggplant, corn cobs
chili peppers my son prizes
but will never eat.
I harvest mescalin greens
pinch out the tiny white flowers
prolong their life.

Nothing tells me it is ready to die
the zucchini still send yellow fruit
from their flowering horns
tomatoes hold fast to the vine
wait on the sun's diligence
the slugs multiply
slide out from under the tall grass
come evening when
shade casts its long arm
over the half raked beds.

I could almost give up my past
at a time like this
the days warm
the garden true to its ardor for me
the nights no betrayal of September's
fickle thumb.
I could become something different
something almost unremembered
something new
desert my father's glass eye that grinds

lust into sand flies
burns holes in the carpet grass
exile his orphaned heart
that never used all its nine lives
but sank here.

If all of life flies like the white duff of fireweed
strewn in the wind
can I forget my name
the lists I have staked
the hard soles of my shoes
and hold to a promise
greater than the seasons flux
greater than the past's hold on me?

The man on the bus

sinks into the tabloids
trolls for love
keeps one hand pressed over
the side of his face.
A scattering of purple kisses
sweep up around his right eye
behind his ear
where God's lips pressed too long and hard
on the birth table
but he has forgotten this
knows only the way life reigns in
what it cannot bathe.

The hemlocks in our backyard could hide the man
a toy water pistol, our child's frisbee
not let them go.
Some things vanish before we realize
they have been waiting for us.

Can money buy everything that offends
erase God's high strung kisses
wield health, elegance, certainty
that the righteous will prevail
will the man on the bus wake up
unpetaled one day?

I dig out old spoons, a rusted canary
pocket pen
things the world forgets
to which the hemlock cling.

For as long as I can remember

you have wanted to dine with me
waxwing my life
into another kind of constituency
as if I am a girl with lust
littering her lips
deft sanctimonials
a battened dress
ready to slide off
into the ripe sleeve
of your tongue.

I make a beeline for hair nets
even hems
the carefully sewn deliverance
calypso orchids that never dry up
always turn the other cheek
tuck their enthusiasms into
the vase's cramped skin.

It is August.
You always hunger for what's
been lost
unsatisfied girls
string beans really
who refuse to let
their defeated loves
cramped shoes
speak for them.

You stir the soup on the side stove.
Encourage me to taste and test.
Add cilantro, beets
dead apparitions I have strung from my past

as if we can go on like this forever
collapsing words
surreptitious lawns
tight houses
pinning paper fans to the trees
mapping fireflies
red lanterns
in the midst of such thirst.

PART FIVE

Tiny Wings on her Fingers

Girl cloaked in thin cotton

chenille toe shoes
in love with the least remembered sunset
sheep on the roof
the stranger who barely knows her
rehearses the moon for her bed.

She remembers back.
The weight of your hands.
Eyes the color of blue geese calling.
How she bent the lampposts around midnight
dangled lavender sachets
let you lathe her body
in bird pecked kisses
till she could not look away.

Winter settles in with its sopping lawn
ice rails, gutters that won't drain.

At one time she would have scaled buildings
honeycombed houses
to live in the curved arm of your love.
But that was before the locusts set in
groomed your hands around other kinds of machinery.
Now you devour the field, lap up clover
the shed's split wood, the sky's empty
her worn down plea.

Girls in thin cotton sully
the wind's deft tongue
the ice storm's imperialism
with their worn down dresses
summer flecked faces
secret placards of Jesus
burning.

We puncture the orange all over

make holes in its skin
so the cloves can hive
breath a scent that will live past
November's cold palms.

My daughter disdains time, believes
you can't buy a wristwatch
for happiness.
My son is twelve. Goes to a school
that runs on precise wheels.
In the store he examines pocket watches
sport versions with graphed dials.
He pushes another clove into the orange.
His sister winds her finger in twists
of bright thread.

I wonder about the scintillation of marriages
the climate of them
when the weather turns red
and every day is a scrape your car
iced window kind of affair.

We breath holiday into the parlor's
stenciled peonies, paper chain the walls.
My daughter wants to string cranberries
set up a corner laden with fairy candles
white chocolate mice
a globe with snow falling.

She will turn the other cheek to keep God
stumbling around for the safety of her door.

Your hands are so big they can
cleave bread, eat up the day's epistles
saunter around in the dark
as if your body mourns for you.
I seal envelopes with tiny notes.
They are for anonymous suitors
the ones who might not walk away
not men with casual eyes and pants
that betray the quotient
of stray birds in them.

I apostrophe everything

wear a round button with *maybe*
no abrupt clauses, declarative sentence
staple my life to the icon of God
gone past bleeding.

It makes no sense to rock salt winter.
My husband tells me that.
His big hands forklift the snow
my children launch their bodies
onto their wood sleds.
They don't know I am a clear a pool
their father won't learn how to swim in.

I gather choke berries for winter's lost thumbs
knit every color of scarf for him.
Maple syrup my days with my love
which never runs smooth
nor pragmatic as smart men.

We are deft with winter
that invisible ice palace
you carve for me
in the snow.

If I cloak the world

in the apothecary of want
bend puddles that muddy the rain
will the eye of God look back
betrothed to a faint light in me
hammer some morse code into the
night's squat air?

Nothing tastes as cruel as the clotheslines
of the past bleeding
the sight of my mother trailing loneliness
under her cotton shift.

All grown up I worship the snow
pocket the wind to keep
the world from mauling
hang swollen thorns from a disused tree
watch God's eye ride steam press
over every weak thing.

You tell me to take hold
proselytize my past
make a mission statement of the
world's bright coins.

I stir soup
pack lunch boxes
martyr my children's love for me.
They are damp with dew
the hope of handrailing snow
to every blank yard.

It is November

I want to cut the wind loose
feel your hands
not picture perfect smelling of jasmine
but age inspired
knotty, distressed as the pine planks
of a well tread floor.

You ask me to hydrant the night
with my pink tongue
as if I am the dollop of some pleasure
the world withholds to which
your hands cling.

I want to make a pact with heaven
four queens and a lucky ace
you stay by my side
decide to hive here
never let me go you say
and keep squeezing my waist.

I stay glued as loyal cotton
the tabernacle of hope
hang on tenuous as autumn apples
the bright coin in your pants
the bright red in my cheeks
before the grass stains them.

A stranger lives in my shoes

I want to wake to the sound of gulls
my mother painting the lines of her love
a man whose hands are candlelight
can lead me out of the rain.

My uncle Truro drowned in the waters
below the Staten Island Bridge
lifted his head to God's notebooks
let his legs slip from under him.
That was forty-five years ago after the war
when I was just a gleam in my papa's eye
when the teller job at the bank
groomed house in the suburbs shrank so small
uncle couldn't see his face.
Three kids my papa later told me
such a selfish man.

The winter here is a glove with ice in it.
We split shovels trying to clean the drive
bury the sides in snow walls so deep my legs vanish.
It is early December, my cousins come by
we cut up paper chains the color of money
tack them onto our parlor wall
my mother dances the tarantella
then vanishes away.

I worship the snow
clear emptiness of it
the way it lands impartial over every damp trespass
round and harsh thing
makes a white refuge on my tongue
dissolves there.

It is Late

The day is an onion skin
with too many layers.
My husband's hands are big
as steam trains
wire fence lines.
You can get lost in them
or be scratched for life.

Some people are so porous
the rain seeps through.
They are as lovely as the
lean trunks of birch trees
the wind courts with its
swollen September tongue.
To break their boughs is to wish
one hundred years of bad luck.

My husband has big hands.
A sterling mind that approves
the mirror image of itself.
I hunker down.
Hear the chainsaw revving.
Spare him the bad luck which was
about to descend on him.

Become a triumph of birch trees.
Walk away in the night's cool pause.

He said she had wings on her fingers

tiny ones
that splashed etudes out of the
piano's cold keys.
She wanted her fingers blank after that
no gold ring, rapt feathery composure
lawn service with its penchant for promising
weedless in a stultified world.

The seasons began to run into each other
with mucked feet.
She dragged her silk stockings off
sang to the garden's initiatives
zucchini plants, pumpkin vine
tomatoes that asked for little
yet offered so much in the face
of her daily allegiance.

She didn't tell anybody that she was
afraid of the sound of her hands
wondered if peril can teach us something
the uncertainty of it
the way it sometimes takes a pulverized being
to release herself
tentatively set sail.

He would say sayonara
leave her alone in a field of tar paper
not because he wanted it that way
but because desire purges the heart
makes loyalty an old shoe with glass in it.

She would see the writing on the wall
the crystal globe of his continence
the way want disturbs every rapt thing.

At that point does the story end
or begin
will she walk her way through madness
with a faint grin
will winter find her
stalking the new snow
remembering every lost thing
that has ever claimed her?

February comes.
She no longer sits in a minefield
by the window seat's refrain
collapses the moon on her tongue
the caveat of happiness
tied to his sleeves.

Paw prints litter the snow.
A scherzo begins to play.
She buys a decent coat
red galoshes
knows it will take all of herself
to be here.

I will not be paraded

as a dancing princess in small feet
nor as the navigable woman
who never lurks in alleys
pronounces only polemics
casts out the wind.

Does there come a time when
inertia breeds us
stasis of how many lost thorns
my cousin Trinity's irreducible
sermons towing.
She has polished feet
words with gills
keeps her purse clutched close
on every train.

I have congregated a host
of thinkers to shed light
Tolstoy with his frozen thumbs
Hesse pruning hedges in the hermitage
Rilke removing himself from even the dog
Dickinson darning socks in the white room
Neruda - such pains over the eggplant,
the garlic's sharp tongue.
They answer me in scarce words
parade life as a soiled coin
with many sides.

You think I'm still your little girl
imbecilic at keeping the flies at bay
managing the house, bank accounts
as if something has gone missing in my head

and I am left with just a handful
of loose leaves
the day's strict discourse
over the roses.

I shall not make amends.
Shall not.
Swelled as an acorn
leave me here impregnated
with my own vices
almost Desdemona
as I mangle
in and out of the fern.

Part Six

Jewels on a Serpent Ring

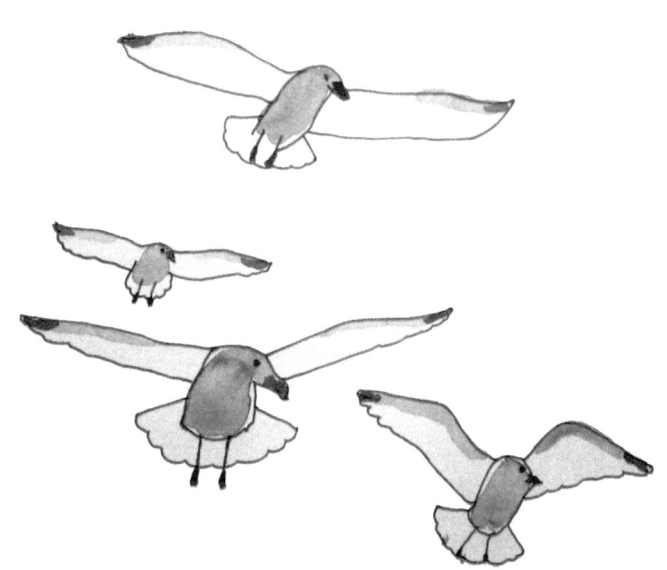

We paper chain loops of colored paper

sandwich words on the inner sleeves of them -
halvah   butterbaby   hickory cup   blue Ebenezer.
Who can be sure what the language of children
will bring to us.
November pressed in dried leaf, aroma of cotton.
You stir honey into my tea water
spread shortbread, stubby delicate fans
across the willow's blue plate.

My children are guessing my age again
older than papa   forty five   they say.
I roll my head back and forth
as if numbers have escaped
remember my ageless mother dancing
atop her funeral pyre
naked in red shoes.

Winter is an anvil between hope and regret.
Your hands are gulls set loose in the dark.
Each night we become a shy nest of kisses
strangers then lovers
in order to see each other rightly in our bed.

I stir basil into the soup pot.
Impregnate my children with braided bags
castoff clothes, hairpins, Russian stories
last year's yarrow
names we try on to replace the used ones.

The parlor grows paper chained with our words
as if diffidence holds no sway here
*magpie   disobedience   bulb   battery   beatitude
begonia   bessoming   mistletoe*
the lamps turned up for the evening meal.

I imagine your hands
how they will come to me
out of nowhere
like wintering sparrows
flutter of wing
land on me
a prayer shawl
heavy as good bread.

I staple cotton

to the room's loose teeth
resurrect my grandmother's quilt
lavender, silk spun out of better days
lay out the sheets with the pregnant holes
lace lipped edge.

Your eyes are the color of sea merchants
that wander over the town's cramped streets
are the blue of mussels, the sea's hold.
I can tell you are a man of hasty voyages
a galley kitchen, keyholes.

One day you will come to me
damp with April
my pantry pressed in garlic, jars of pimento
powdered plums, apricots saved in a box.
My children will weep the gold coin
of your return
the delicate white hands you have
saved for us.

All day I row between Marissa
and the sea
scaffold want, dissolution
till they are a park bench
seeded with pigeons.
My earrings tipped with the weight
of your love.

I want to dance
but my feet have eloped
in your shoes.

We dollop whipped cream

onto our pancakes
as if there is no tomorrow
no shark attack that can rattle
the puff cakes of children.

It is February.
Everything I thought I ever knew
escapes me.
The children drown their pancake
in the juice of cherries.
My husband's hands estimate the rain.
Two dogs wait on crumbs
beneath the table.

How can I tell the world
I have wed a forked tongue
that decency hangs squat
on a pared down tree?

We initial our past.
Spell snow into the arms of the wind.
Load ourselves with hats, gloves,
nubby scarfs
as if the tire gutted roadway
cramped house
my mother's early dismissal
can be erased
like the woman who white powders her face
camouflages dark circles
till she is the unpummeled hill calling.

It is February.
The past can't hurt me anymore.

Back in Yevsky you came to me

clear light on a purgatoried day
the lavender clothe of it
pot of black tea
words that scatter their thimbles
grow warm as watermelon seeds
then walk away.

I confess to you that
I have left my mother with no shoes.
She is old and I worry about her
in her scant blue coat
the sermon of crows calling.
Delinquent child lost amid
the market stalls, fish grinding
machinery.

How many bodies have frozen to death
in a house with thin walls?

Some people believe that death
is an overgrown garden
and what we don't tend
dries up in infirmed hands
that there is derision in the doilies
the walnut sideboard coated in dust so thick
my mother wrote her name.

The tableau of want
my Aunt Gelbhur says
has invaded our beds.
She swears by her crystal rosary
hulks her flour sack of repentance into the street
looks for miracles

shakes her head over
the men who have spent the weight
of their bodies over the delicacy
of my mother's bed.

I am back at the table with you
mourning America, the headlines
my misshapen hands.
You pour more tea
offer up saffron buns from a
scallop edged dessert plate
the sermon of praise that belies
what we spend.

I dream of spoons, no heart failure
my thrifty father
lighting the oil lamp
my mother guardian of fishes
the discourse of your hands
balm of the eucalyptus tree
the tamer of serpents
how they rise and descend on me
carry my clearest envelopes
my body's softest effigies
her quivering voice
here and abroad
back home again.

You keep track

of what we have here
no longer bead worry over whether
it migrates away.
The tomato and relish
pressed tight between the bread's snug kisses
the tyrant of want pinned up to dry
a bleached white blouse
on the tightrope of clothesline.

There are deliberate shoes
that go anywhere in a harsh wind
eat up the sand, fever the dark
never defeat themselves
over the tyranny of our
oil slicked gaze.

Words have a habit of crowding in on me
like buildings that pile up
in an over endowed city.
At idle times I split seams, rake mud
open envelopes with paper cranes.

One day maybe nothing will fit
my breath will be a wide arm of sky
punctuated with birds.
I will stop eating, grow long
tapered as the yard's pole beans.

Will the night refuse to forget me
remember the shape of my hips
your prescription to tap terrestrial
out of every drowned child
lost seed?

When I go through the chronicles

of my life
will I find you there
listening for meadowlark
bronzed by the sun's devotion
the rain's slick tongue
mining the allegiance of tiger lily
lady slipper
cucumbers small as thumbnails
spreading their unhinged burden
along the vines clear spine?

Will you call me delinquent
a slow learner
girl with rocks in her shoes
who must count, recount the sums
call into question the obduracy
of the roses
as if there are unspoken handrails
to heaven
and every being is more than the congruence
the world lends?

It is July.
There are less rocks in my shoes.
Less shoes.
I counterbalance the weight of the world
with my blue notebooks
your insistence I tap terrestrial
out of the day's loose keys.
My children play string games
dip in and out of the wade pool
collect rocks
chipped overlooked ones

spill them onto the yard's table
pile them, balance them, pocket them
disregard them, regard them
carve them with their unceremonious hands.

Is this world they live in
an agreeable place
the rocks being the rocks
but then more than the rocks
fabric of pyramids, totems
stone towers where girls wait
to let down their meander of hair
this summer being this summer
July in the middle of a heat wave
the translucent beetle
you being everywhere
climbing in and out of the easy
avenue of our hands?

Summer sits with its dry tongue

its desire to press pink into the bed sheets
warden the garden's repose.
I stay out late night
remember the curse of love that once hived
in my bed
the men who could never find me
tractless as the missiles of happiness
that leave dead skin in the sand.

You have hands so big
I could lose myself
have an airtight version of paradise
catalog the world
a technician
in charge of the delicacy of lace.

Will we grow old together with adjacent tongues
will I climb the ladder of a paradise
so durable you can't see me anymore
is the world as much thistle as wisteria
calamine as clove weed?

The earth tells me July has a groundswell
of miracles to lend
moles pile dirt high as cemetery mounds
geranium you passed for dead
come back one small leaf at a time
the patapan squash, tomatoes, corn
escape the fate of the cabbage heads
the neighbor's formidable spray can
remain ungutted by the slugs' voracious.

I stockpile my past like tiny jewels
on a serpent ring
remember the gifts of it
the wide arm of heaven
the way God keeps riding ramrod
over every deft thing.

Morning is an arm of light

so hazardous the birds won't flock.
I dig migration out of my pants sleeves
abandon the ancient philosopher, Dako,
who said *to wander is an act of treason*
so faithful, it brings the mercy of wings
to your gate

stop wandering
stay stapled in one place
stumble in darkness
as if darkness contains me
my green speckled eggs
the eye the tree protects
amid the night's pitch black insignia.

You will come to me
on a day that digresses from this one
wear your scuffed mourning slippers
mismatched combs
my garden a timphony
hillsides of wild geranium
skunk cabbage
foxglove raising their spire of bells.

I am almost unassailable now in my blue skirt
the cut and paste version of paradise
my children hold.
They roll down hills
forget there is a tomorrow, bruised apples
only the blackberries' bright stain
your body mapping the distance
tall summer grass burning.

Precocious girl

the Torah loves you along with
the incandescent epistles.
Jesus through the looking glass is *not* dead.
Nor your camisole, nylon stockings
with the river of back seams.
Umbrella hope and it becomes
something to live by
pure as Beatrice's calendula soap
your mother with her pearl stickpins
able to anchor heaven
temporarily to her head.

Lord do not make me a crucible of
the day's lost shoes
nail only navigable journeys
to my breath
help me see that what is crushed
always comes back to us
in jade slippers
if not in this life
then in the next one
or the next
or the next
you have bequeathed
for me.

Part Seven

Perfect Pantomime

At 8pm I will meet my lover

he stockpiles compost for our yard
meet him in front of the French café
between Belmont and Stark.
He will anguish over the world's breaking
obsess about the day's indictments
bombings in London, Egypt
Oregon budget that won't pass.
I will ply baked brie into his mouth's damp wing.
The waiter will be lean as a runner
cute with his nipped pants
watery blue eyes.

It's 90 degrees
the restaurant has no air conditioner
my dress will stick to my thighs
tight as a pear waiting to be peeled.

I will want to offer a prism
for what's been lost
imagine the two of us wandering
along the Champs Elysees
a choir of birds in my hand
my love not sanguine but crusty
as a loaf of good bread, soft and dense
when you dig in with your teeth.

It will be approaching midnight
the city lights spread across an unhinged sky.
We won't be weary, need to drive anywhere
will know only the steady bird peck of kisses
the wafer of happiness
love calls back into our arms.

Lucky in love the cards tell her

as if she has no epistemological flags towing
and any man can carry her
past her mother's grave
seed her in a house with balanced window boxes
neat geranium
bleak fences
reliable children who spell diligence
out of the terrible certainty of their days.

Someone leaks quinine into her grape juice
a cankerous past
a man who cannot see her through the rain
as if she's lopsided, archaic even
her opus of driftwood, unspoiled thread,
the gilded eye of the world calling.

You have a habit of untangling rope lines.
She doesn't know it
is posed on the verge of indecency
examines her words, the slope of your pink tongue
your big hands that spackle the moon
gather foxglove, thistle, wild geranium
take hold of her waist
do not walk away.

Six days and six nights they say it takes
to create a new world
populate it with ridges, fish fused rivers
the ambling plain
every animal the inventive eye can offspring
six days, six nights to draw you
into her bed
a steamed bun of undecipherable ingredients.

She leaves off eating ordinary meat after that
no longer pilfers the pantry
acts the piranha in cut away shoes

becomes a Parisian tart of complex experience
stalks of sugar cane
testifies to the fact that anything is possible
in the wide mouth
of your beckoning.

How many times has my good luck ring

saved
pulverized winter
with its wolfbane
corded wood missing.
I am proselytizing through hard country
rough terrain with my pitted boots
sullied map.
My mother looks on with her halted breath
pressure cooks the night
sends me arm loads of wheat
sorghum cakes
fights off dissonance with her blue stick.

All day I find myself rowing toward heaven
plying the water in my leaf mulch boat.
Even the mustard greens notice
my pockmarked ascendancy.

They say God blisters every rapt thing
scalds the tongue of sinners
til they can barely speak
that sometimes we must go blind
in order to see again.

I let my hands lead.
Cup tomatoes, eggplant
nuzzle the beet leaves
stumble over rocks, winter's prairie of rain
find something wordless, small
barely imaginable
you have left for me.

You lead with your lusts flailing

My father once told me that.
Propositioned me to hold fast
to my words
anchor them
like spindly cousins on an irksome
clothesline
become the tactful girl
with no treasons.
I foster silence
wade in tepid water
till it is waist high
almost drowns me
arrives clear up to my head.

Now I hold court over every shrill thing
slug colonies, bug eaten cabbage
lawn erupted mole hills
betray only the wind
watch the world eat itself to death
with a guileless hand.

There are poisonous mushrooms
in our backyard
colonies of clover
fences with unmanageable paint peel.
I stockpile my past
unbutton time with its tight pants legs
remember my mother
who made a field day out of nothingness
the bee's swarm

the nasturtium multiplying willy nilly
below her yard swing
the bracelet she made of the world's loose teeth
gathered and threaded
without any ambush of shade.

Summer sits

a commotion of bare feet.
You eschew promises.
Say they have no anchor
are a hairpin boat in a wind lashed sea.

She walks on tapioca
the craters the moon thrusts
with buried life.
You threaten to come across to her bed.
She has never been alive in her own skin.

Her feet beside the lamppost
begin to rise
the creosote tips of them
till everything is tantamount to morning
its blue promise

the way two beings can cut themselves loose
fly.

When my Prince Comes He will be Fast as Lightning

I won't eat dulse anymore
squander my refrigerator magnets
the fishnet stockings yanked up over my knees
snowflake version of paradise pawing.

The porcelain headed dolls will wander out
of their blue cages
suck sunlight, lemon ices, pick field daisy
find the sorrel hidden behind the pond shed.
My pump heels that were last will be first
perfect pantomime of the days remembrance
muffled song of the finch
turning our clump of cedar
away from gianthood
into sweet sleep.

I will rest
with my painted tail
with your hands that carry the wind
plant seeds, pestilence, saffron
into my dimly lit places.

And I will love you with everything
my tongue was made for
no longer waxen, tired old soul
but young girl weaving the long legs of daisy
paradox of thistle
into a bower for your hair.

Prince pregnant with fallenness
you mount the tall hill that enters my door.

If you eat a perfect peach

its succulence stays with you forever.

I have eaten a perfect peach
stumbled along the handrails to heaven
found a pitch so dissonant it carries the rain.

In Fargo, North Dakota the ground
freezes up for months
winter turns water into ice ponds.
Wind swaggers the lonely rope on the bells.
To be risen is to be in my mother's palm.
She weaves a new map out of loneliness
hallelujahs it with my saved hands.

They say a girl who is hungry enough
can sponge up the dark
skate past certainty
lure faith to her bed.
I paint fireflies, practice penance
emblem my life to the color of mercy
bake cake, steam pudding.
My mother lays out blue Wedgwood
gathers the birds.

Spring returns.
No longer the absentminded stranger
you straddle hope
worship the silt and silk
of my body's estuaries.

In October I will marry you when the jewels hang on the leafless tree

Taffeta and lace
honeycombs
caterpillar clad jewel box
of the beveled tree.
Everything shivers
with happiness
when autumn's red tongue
claims.

Things already lost
come back
my love with his crumpled
blue shirt
whitewashes the rain.

I could spit
at the moon
making me wait this long
for the jewels that hang
on the leafless tree
or thank the fortune teller
my lucky stars
for the sight of you

your hands that hover
over me
swollen with bee sting
my bed dripping
of honey
risen bark
of the bough's exuberance.

Toni Thomas lives in Portland, Oregon. Her poems have appeared in literary magazines in Austria, Spain, New Zealand, Canada, England, Scotland, and Australia. In the United States her work has been accepted for publication in over fifty literary magazines, including Prairie Schooner, North Dakota Quarterly, Hayden's Ferry Review, the Minnesota Review, Weber-The Contemporary West, Rhino, Notre Dame Review, and Poetry East.

She has published five other poetry collections – *Chosen, Walking on Water, Ace Raider of the Unfathomable Universe, Blue Halo* and a chapbook *Fast as Lightning*. Her work has received numerous awards and twice been nominated for a Pushcart Prize.

When she is not teaching or writing poems Toni enjoys sculpting clay. Her figurative pieces have been shown in gallery and museum exhibits in Portland and Chicago, displayed in literary magazines, and housed in private collections in the U.S. and England.

Since Toni remains buried in poems and manuscripts, she likes to imagine all of them out in the world thick as wild lupin swaying.

She can be contacted at www.tonithomaspoetry.com

www.ingramcontent.com/pod-product-compliance
Lightning Source LLC
Chambersburg PA
CBHW020619300426
44113CB00007B/701